PANANANDATA ROPE FIGHTING

Amante P. Marinas, Sr.

PANANANDATA ROPE FIGHTING

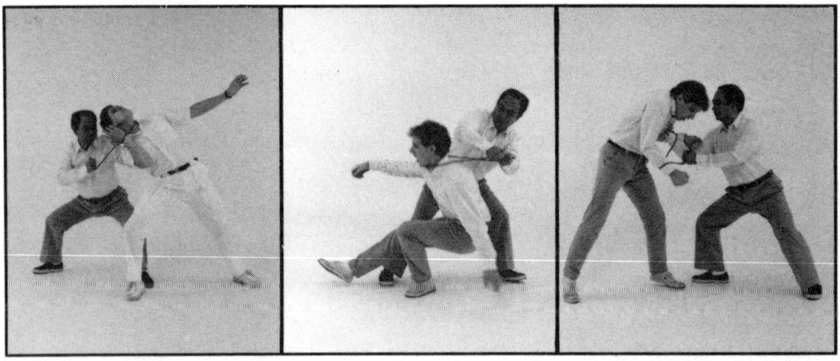

Filipino Choking and Binding Techniques

PALADIN PRESS
BOULDER, COLORADO

Other books by Amante P. Marinas, Sr.:

Pananandata Knife Fighting
Pananandata Yantok at Daga: Filipino Stick and Dagger

Pananandata Rope Fighting:
Filipino Choking and Binding Techniques
by Amante P. Marinas, Sr.

ISBN 0-87364-494-8
Printed in the United States of America

Published by Paladin Press, a division of
Paladin Enterprises, Inc., P.O. Box 1307,
Boulder, Colorado 80306, USA.
(303) 443-7250

Direct inquiries and/or orders to the above address.

Contents

Dedication

To my grandparents, Cirilo Marinas and Pilar Marcelo, and Alejo Paclarin and Maria de Sahagun.

Acknowledgments

I am indebted to Robert Rivera, a student and a friend, whose initial questions about the use of the *lubid* (rope) led to the writing of this book. It is Robert Rivera and another student, Robert Mulligan, who provided me with the necks, arms, ribs, and knees to test the sequences of techniques and cut them down to the essential minimum.

I would like to thank Andre Lubart, a dedicated student, for his assistance during the photography sessions.

I owe many thanks to Bert Caoile, whose usual patience and excellent photographs made the writing of the text less difficult.

This book could not have been completed without the help of my wife, Cherry, and my son, Mat, Jr., whom I asked to become attackers when I had doubts about my techniques.

About the Author

Amante P. Marinas, Sr., studied pananandata with Ingkong Leon Marcelo and arnis one-stick fighting with Grandmaster Porferio S. Lanada. Marinas is a former professor of chemical engineering at Adamson University in Manila, Philippines.

Marinas was awarded the Master rating in arnis on April 12, 1987. He holds black belts in shorin ryu (Commando Karate Club) and aikido (Philippine Aikido Club). He was introduced to pananandata in 1948.

He has authored five other books: *Arnis de Mano, Arnis Lanada Book 1, Pananandata Knife Fighting, Pananandata Yantok at Daga,* and *Pananandata Dalawang Yantok.* He is the most published practitioner of the Philippine martial arts and is the only person teaching pananandata in the United States.

He is originally from Pambuan, a small barrio in Gapan, Nueva Ecija, Philippines. He speaks Tagalog. Today, Marinas lives in Queens, New York, with his wife, Cherry, and son, Mat, Jr.

Preface

The rope is a common enough item to be available in any emergency. Its variants include twine used for tying packages, colored ribbons, chains, ties, and belts. The rope and its variants have a common use: to fix something in place.

The rope can tie up an attacker's hands or feet. In extreme cases, it can be used to form a noose on the attacker's neck. It can also be used to strike the attacker, but only if the rope is heavy enough. For example, hitting with colored ribbons used to tie packages will not have any effect on an attacker. Tying him up with them, however, will put him in his place.

The rope is a very useful weapon for defense. However, it requires special skill to be able to entwine the attacker's leg, arm, or neck with it. The need for special skill is magnified when dealing with an attacker who is armed with a knife, club, or gun.

No book has yet been written on the use of rope and its variants for self-defense. At best, the rope's use for such a purpose has been presented as a mere collection of tricks—it has never been systematized.

A systematic approach does exist. It can be found

in *pananandata,* a system of fighting taught in the Tagalog regions of Central Luzon in the Philippines. The concepts and methods of pananandata, which include fighting with the empty hand and with bladed or club-like weapons, are here specifically applied to the use of a rope for self-defense.

Basic Concepts

The ease or the difficulty with which you capture an attacker will depend on the weight, length, and dropping characteristics of the rope or its variants, and on your skill.

A heavy rope is ideal for striking, as with a whip. Thrown with enough power, its free end can coil around an attacker's limb. On the other hand, a light rope has to be wielded with better skill to be able to make a capture. For example, the free end of a heavy chain can whip around an attacker's neck. The free end of a light rope might not whip around. Hence, to make a capture with a light rope, you will have to draw a clockwise or a counterclockwise loop around an attacker's neck.

A long rope, while it has certain advantages, will have too much slack. You will have to take up this slack. If the rope is longer than the distance between the centers of your outstretched hands, tugging at its ends will not completely stretch it. There will be some slack left and any attempt to capture an attacker's neck or limb with it will be unsuccessful. At best, the capture will be too slow.

Dropping characteristics—the way a rope freely drops—is associated with the weight of the rope and with the type of material it is made of. Ropes that drop "clean" are ideal for captures. Ropes that don't will need "coaxing." For example, an electrical cord—a copper wire wrapped in insulation—will not whip around and therefore has to be wrapped around the attacker's neck.

Equally important to the ease of capture is your skill. You can have a rope of ideal material, length, weight, and dropping characteristics, but if you lack skill you will not make a capture. For this reason, I have illustrated in detail methods of capture that you can practice to sharpen your skills.

The methods demonstrated in this chapter are used to capture the arm or the neck. Subsequent chapters illustrate methods of capture against a variety of armed and unarmed situations. Dedicated practice will give you the confidence and physical ability to make these captures.

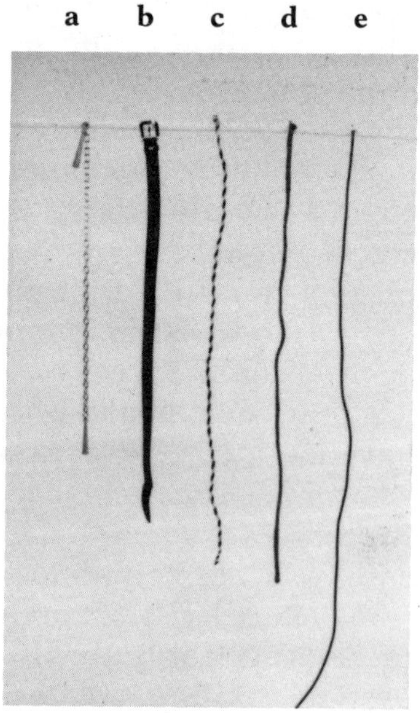

Dropping Characteristics. The chain (a) and the belt (b) drop straight down. The twine (c, d) and the electrical cord (e) do not drop "clean." Dropping characteristics will affect your techniques. Chain (a), belt (b), and twine (d) are used in the following photographs. The chain is 36½ inches long; the belt, 40½ inches; the striped twine, 48 inches; the dark twine, 48 inches; and the electrical cord, 60 inches.

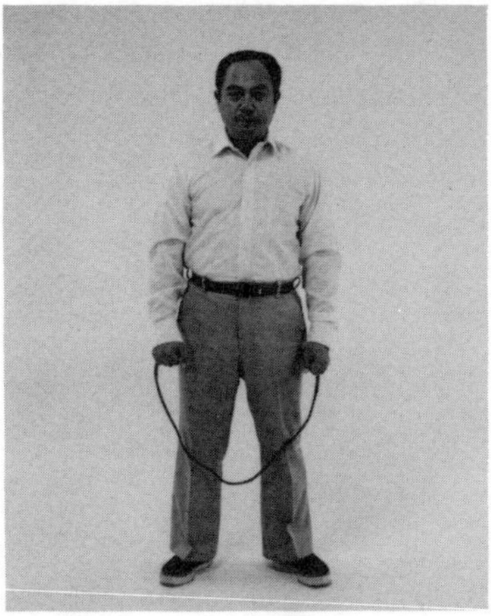

Figure 1

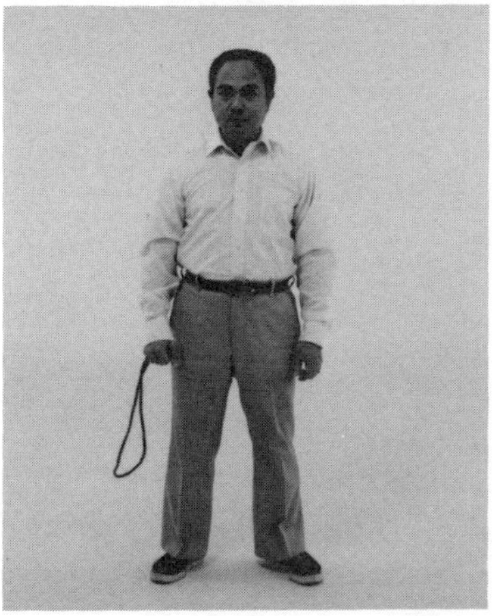

Figure 2

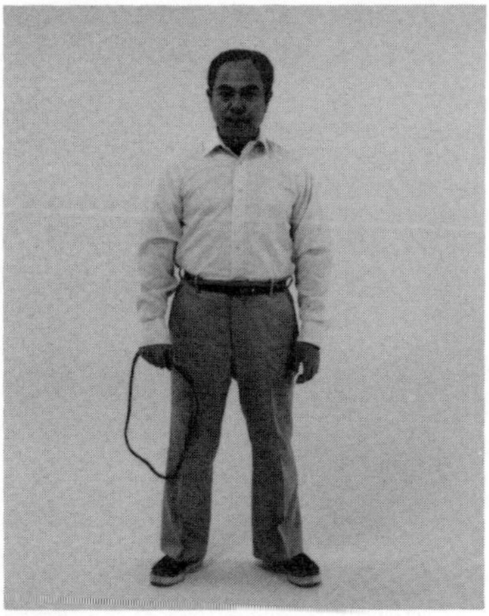

Figure 3

Holding the Rope. The rope may be held with one end in each hand (Figure 1), or with both ends in one hand (Figures 2, 3). In Figure 3, the rope is already looped.

Capturing one arm. Have your partner extend his right arm with a closed fist. Hit his forearm with your right arm (Figure 4). Bring the left end of the rope up (Figure 5), draw a clockwise loop around and over his arm, and backfist to the face (Figure 6).

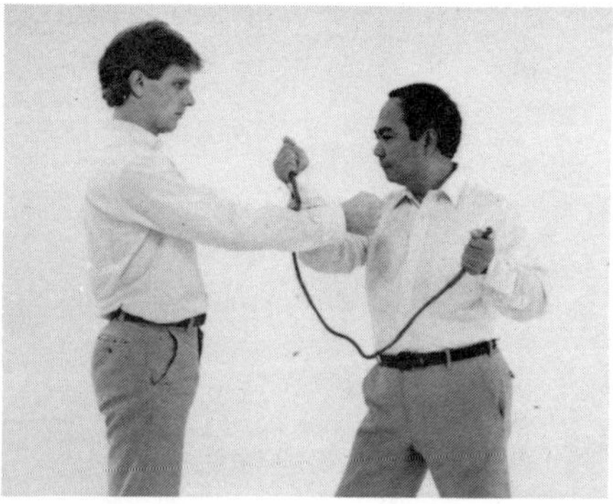

Figure 4

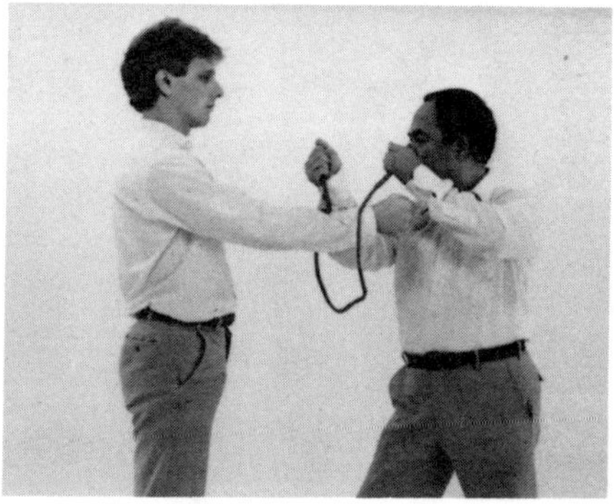

Figure 5

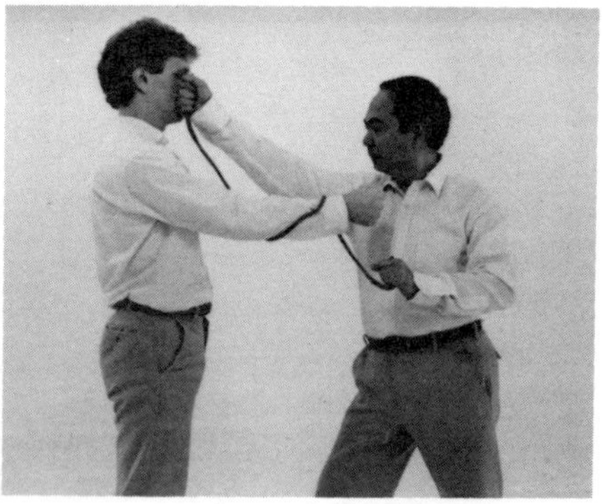

Figure 6

Let your partner grab your arm (Figure 7). Rotate your fist counterclockwise under, then over your partner's wrist (Figures 8, 9). At the end of the rotation, grasp the length of the rope with your right hand to complete the loop (Figure 10).

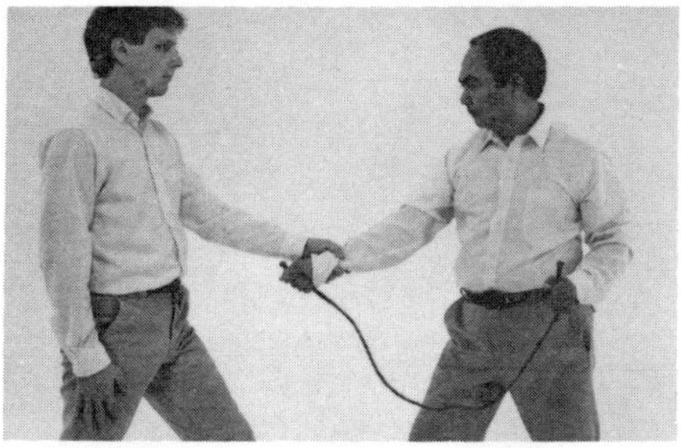

Figure 7

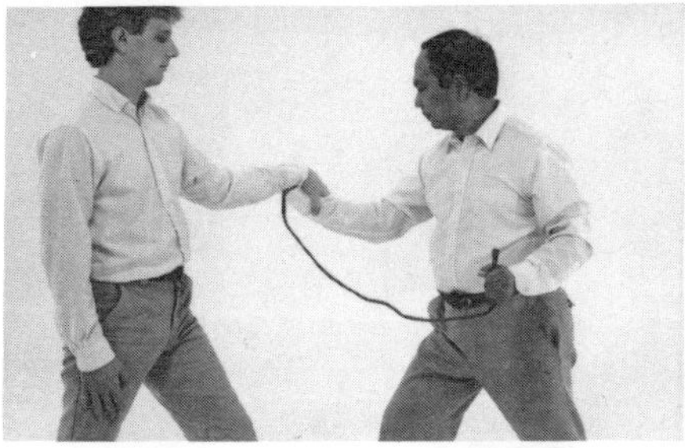

Figure 8

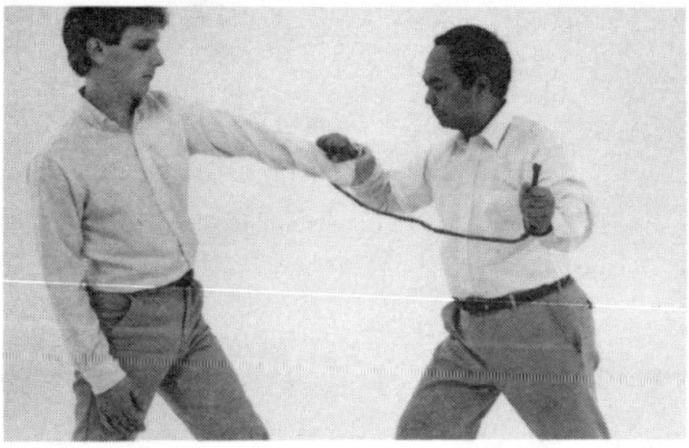

Figure 9

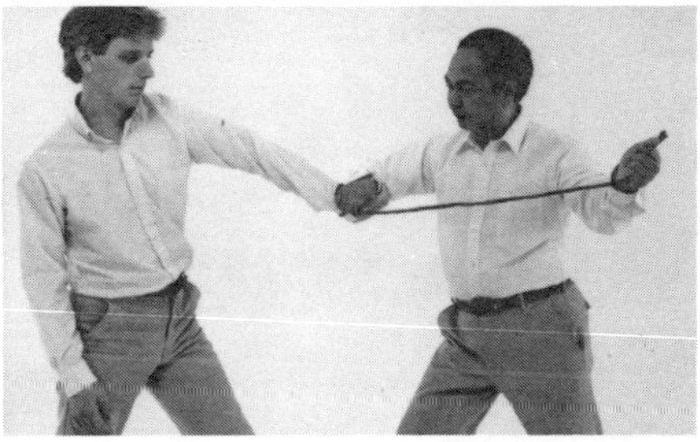

Figure 10

Capturing two arms. Have your partner extend his right fist. Hit his forearm (Figure 11), then start a clockwise loop with the left end of the rope (Figure 12). Simultaneously, complete the loop, pull down with your left hand, and block his left arm with your right arm (Figure 13).

Loop (clockwise) the rope's right end over (Figure 14), then under your partner's left arm (Figure 15). Grasp the two lengths of the rope in the middle (Figure 16).

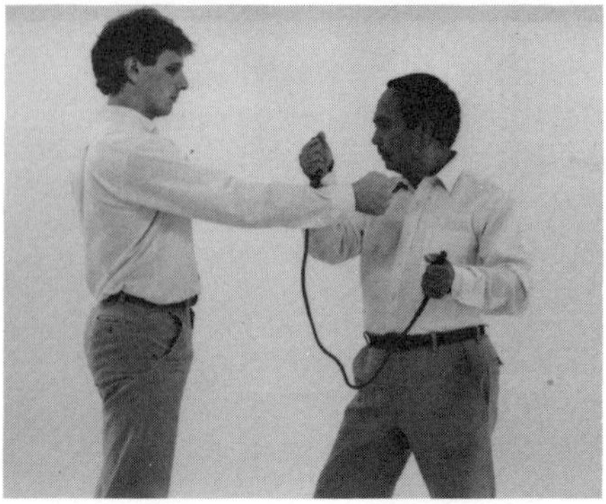

Figure 11

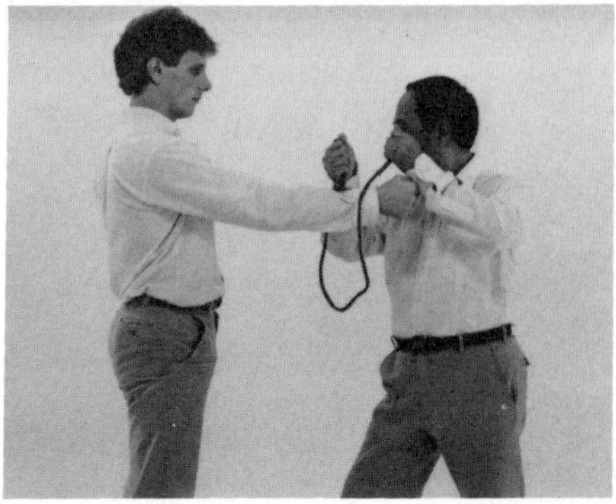

Figure 12

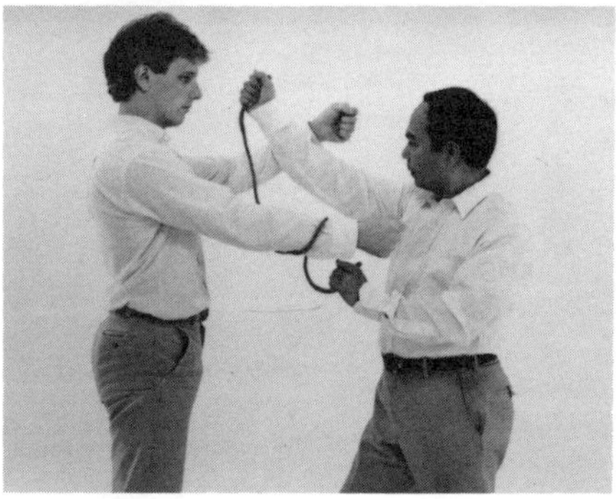

Figure 13

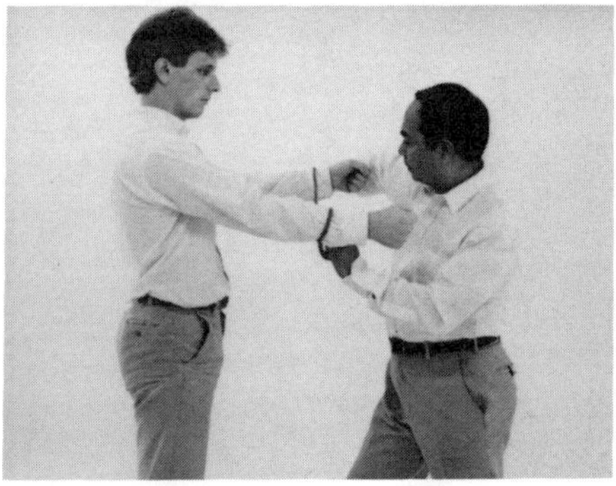

Figure 14

Figure 15

Figure 16

Cutting the arm. Put slack on one end of the rope (Figure 17), then quickly pull the other end tight (Figures 18, 19).

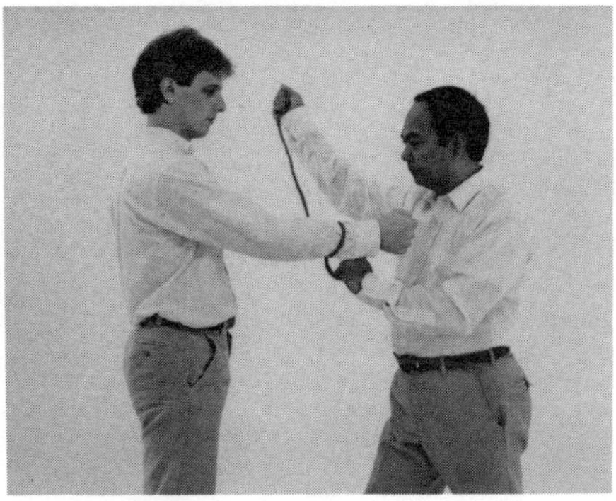

Figure 17

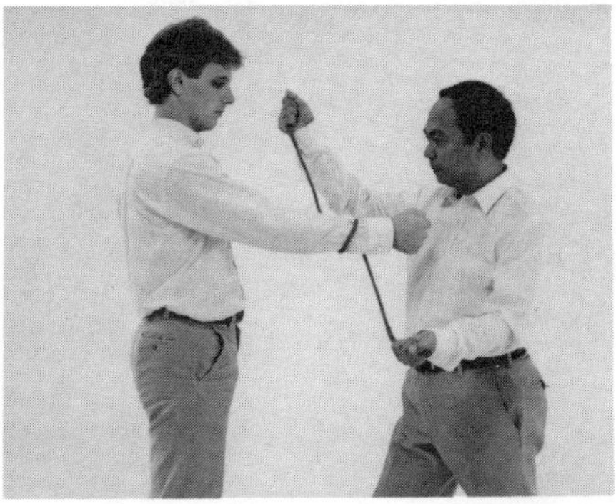

Figure 18

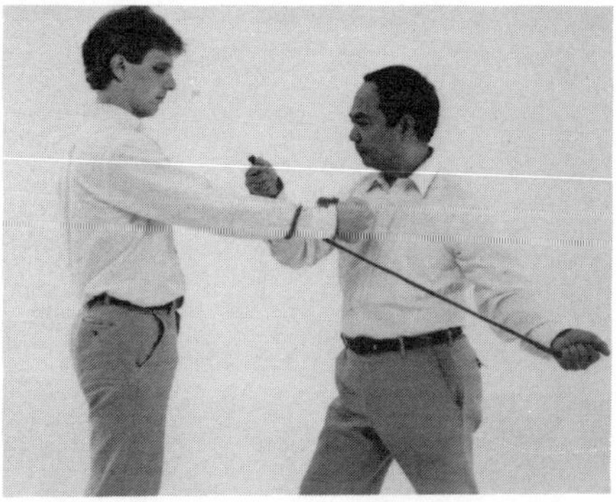

Figure 19

Capturing the weapon arm. Have your partner extend his weapon hand. Block his forearm (Figure 20). At the same time, throw one end of the rope over his forearm and grasp the thrown end with your left arm (Figure 21). Pull down with your left hand (Figure 22).

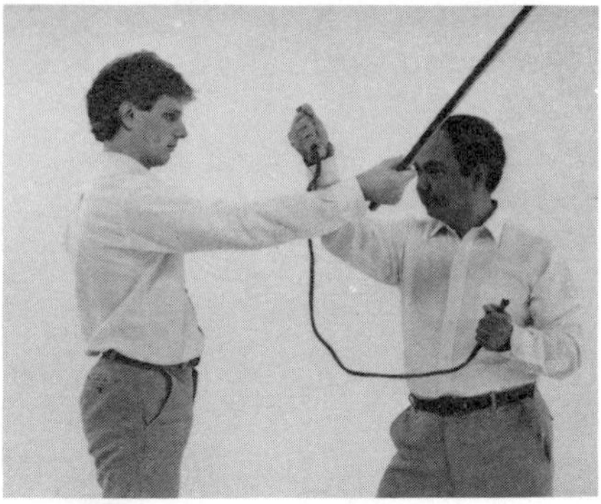

Figure 20

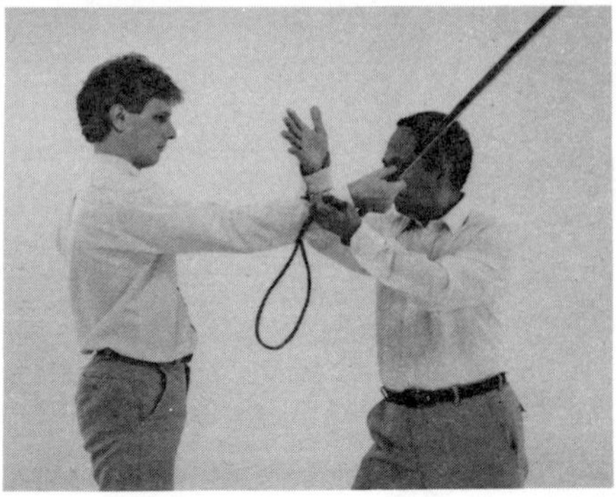

Figure 21

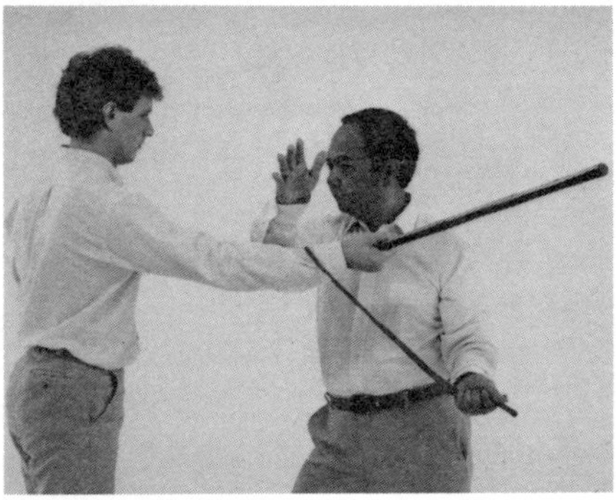

Figure 22

Capturing the neck. Have your partner extend his right fist. Strike his arm (Figure 23). Simultaneously, graze-punch his jaw with your right hand, and hit the base of his right ear with your left hand (Figure 24). These strikes will give you the time to release the left end of the rope and grasp the two ends with your right hand (Figure 25). Capture the neck in a "clothesline" (Figure 26).

Figure 23

Figure 24

Figure 25

Figure 26

Have your partner extend his right fist. Graze-punch the outside of his forearm (Figure 27). Step in with your right foot and throw the rope over his head (Figure 28). This will catch his neck in a clothesline. Step in with your left foot, then pull (Figure 29).

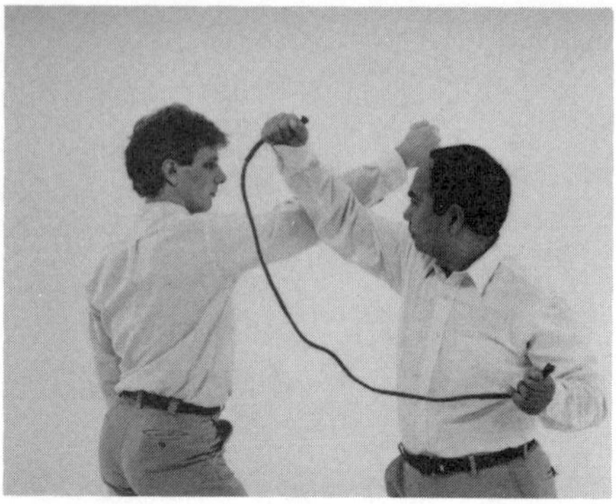

Figure 27

Figure 28

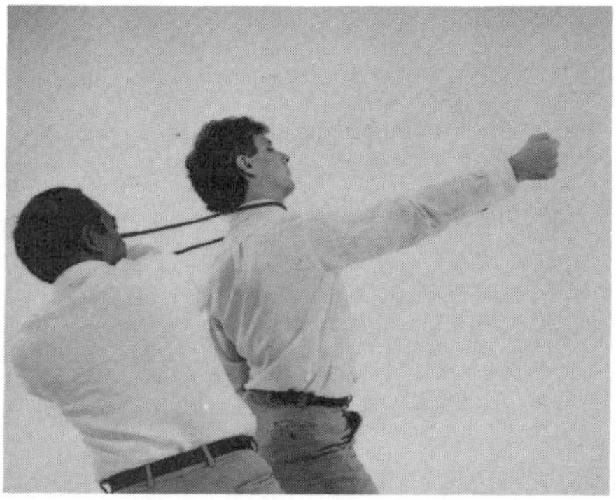

Figure 29

Have your partner lower his head (Figure 30). Draw a counterclockwise loop by bringing the right end of the rope up (Figure 31), over, and around (Figure 32) your partner's neck. Pull both ends tightly to complete the capture (Figure 33).

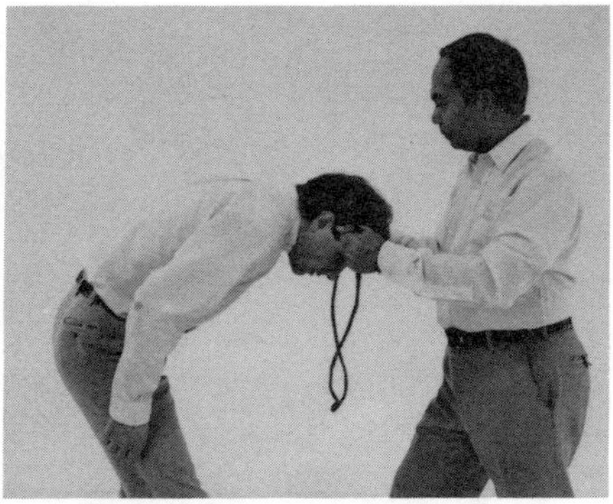

Figure 30

Figure 31

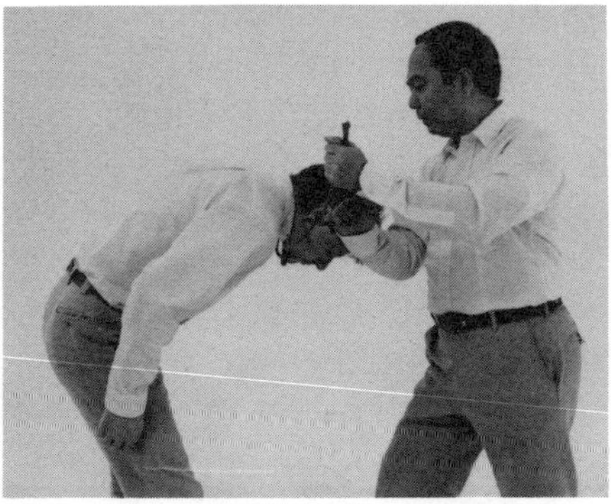

Figure 32

Figure 33

Have your partner lower his head (Figure 34). Draw a clockwise loop by bringing the left end of the rope up (Figure 35), over, and around (Figure 36) your partner's neck. Pull both ends tightly to complete the capture (Figure 37).

Figure 34

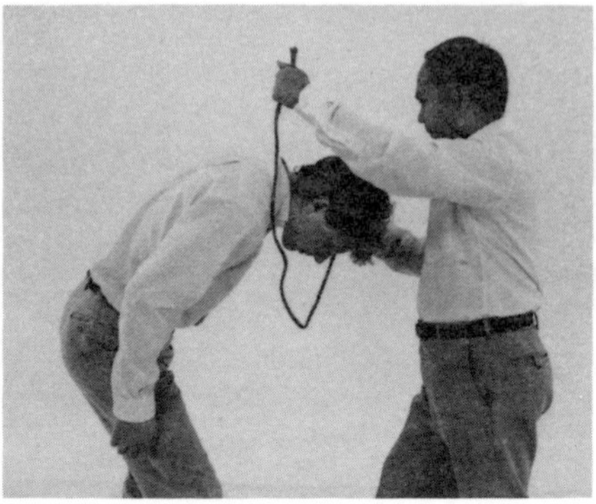

Figure 35

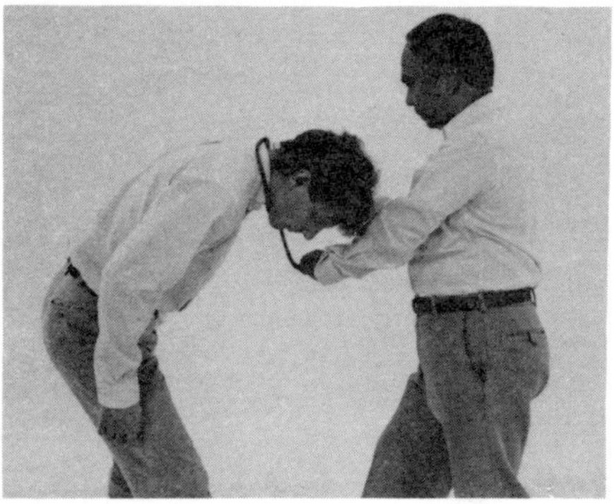

Figure 36

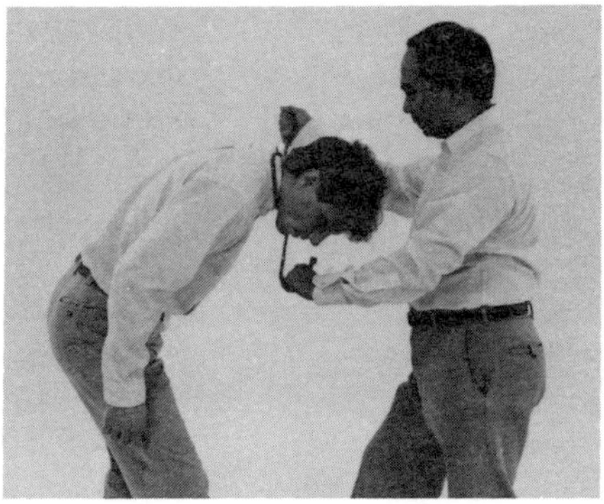

Figure 37

Rope and Chain: Defense Against Empty-Hand, Knife, and Stick Attacks

There are many types of attacks. Hence, if you are to put up a good defense, you must have full knowledge of an attacker's trajectories.

Attacks to the body can be either high or low, downward or upward, from the left or from the right. The attacks can be aimed at the upper and lower left, at the upper and lower right, and at the midsection. Attacks aimed at the lower left or at the lower right can take the form of knife thrusts, punches, or kicks. Attacks aimed at the upper left or upper right can take the form of overhead attacks with club-like or bladed weapons. Similarly, attacks aimed at the midsection can take the form of thrusts with club-like or bladed weapons, or of kicks and punches. These attacks and targets are tabulated below:

SECTION	TARGET	TRAJECTORY
Upper left	top of head	downward vertical
	left shoulder	downward diagonal
	left biceps	horizontal

SECTION	TARGET	TRAJECTORY
Lower left	kidney, groin	upward
Upper right	top of head right shoulder right biceps	downward vertical downward diagonal horizontal
Lower right	kidney, groin	upward
Midsection	stomach solar plexus	frontal frontal

Body targets have to be protected with defensive actions. These actions are a series of movements designed to deal not only with the direction but also the power and speed of an attack. Defensive actions leading to captures will appear complicated. However, they have certain patterns. These are:

1. *A sidestep or an advance at a 45-degree angle, followed immediately by a strike.* The advance or the sidestep will displace the target (part of your body) away from the line of attack. The near-simultaneous strike will break the attacker's concentration and will allow you to place one end of the rope in the proper position for a capture.
2. *A second strike followed by, or simultaneous with, the advance of the rear foot.* The strike will position the other end of the rope for the capture. The advance will further close the distance.
3. *A third strike, simultaneous with grasping the two ends of the rope.* This strike will allow you the time to grasp the two ends of the rope and complete the loop around the attacker's limb or neck.
4. *A sudden pull with the rope.* The sudden pull will bring the attacker down. This should be simultaneous with a sidestep or a back step to lend

power to the technique. At the same time, this will guard against the possibility of the attacker falling on your leg.

5. *A final strike.* The final strike should precede tying up the attacker with the rope.

The rope is a close-quarter weapon. Hence, you need to get close to the attacker to use it effectively.

Several guidelines will help you develop the proper footwork to close the gap. First, all advances or retreats should be at an angle. Advances or retreats to the right should start with the right foot, and those to the left should start with the left foot. Second, because of the need for mobility, the most useful stance is one where most of your body weight is put on the rear foot. Third, you must use short steps so that you can halt your advance or retreat without losing your balance. Fourth, you must disguise your advance by simultaneously attacking either with your hands or your feet.

Captures are made by tying up the arms or the neck. A capture is preceded or accompanied by strikes to stun the attacker long enough so that a loop can be completed.

Capturing is done by drawing a clockwise or a counterclockwise loop with either end of the rope around the attacker's arms or neck. Captures can also be made by throwing one end of the rope around the neck or over the arm. A third method of capture is effected on the head more readily if the rope is already looped.

The length of the rope you are using will determine the ease or the difficulty of a capture. A short rope can capture the arm but not the neck. A forty-one-inch rope, however, can simultaneously capture the arm and the neck. An overly long one, such as a skipping rope, will have too much slack and captures with it will be relatively slow.

Another variable that will affect your technique is the height of your opponent. If you are as tall as he, capturing the neck will present no difficulty. If you are shorter, a kick to the shin or a blow to the body will make the opponent bend his knee and cause him to lower his head. Capturing the arm is only slightly affected by the height of the opponent—if you are shorter, you may have to stretch to the limit of your reach.

One other variable to be considered is the type of rope used. Chains and ropes that drop straight will be excellent for capturing either the neck or the arm. However, you will need better skill to effect the same capture with ropes that do not drop straight.

The most difficult part of the body to capture is the leg. It is easier to capture the head than to capture the hands because, relatively speaking, the head moves less freely.

It is wise to practice with opponents of different heights using ropes with different dropping characteristics. You should also practice with ropes of different lengths and weights. If you normally wear a belt, spend more time practicing with it or with a rope of identical length.

One

In Figure 38, the attacker aims a punch at your face with his right hand. Focus your eyes on the attacker's chest. As he punches, step forward to the right with your right foot. Simultaneously, parry his punch by blocking his forearm with your right arm (Figure 39). Do not advance too far forward. If you do, you will get within striking range of the attacker's left hand. This advance should take you close enough to effect a capture.

By blocking the forearm, you will shock the attacker long enough to prevent him from striking with his left hand. It will also prevent him from kicking with his right foot. The hit on the forearm might not stop the attacker from using his left hand, however. Hence, you must quickly deliver a backfist to his face while simultaneously capturing his right hand with a clockwise loop of the left end of the rope (Figure 40). Take up the slack on the rope, pull taut, and step back with your right foot (Figure 41). This backward step will put the greater part of your body weight on the attacker's captured wrist. It will also prevent the attacker from falling on your leg.

Note that the key to a successful capture of the punching hand is to render it immobile with a quick, powerful strike—in this case, with the right arm block.

Figure 38

Figure 39

Figure 40

Figure 41

Two

In the previous technique, you were able to strike, close the distance, execute the backfist, and complete the loop to capture the attacker's arm. However, there may be times when the attacker might still be able to punch with his free left hand. This can very well happen when your strike to the forearm is neither powerful enough nor fast enough. Also, the attacker might have set you up and *wanted* you to come in.

As the attacker punches (Figure 42), step to the right and hit his left forearm with your right forearm (Figure 43). The left-hand punch can be parried by simply raising your elbow (Figure 44). Practiced often enough, this parry can come in the form of a backfist to the face. The parry is simultaneous with the capture of the attacker's right hand with the left end of the rope.

The right end of the rope is now used to capture the attacker's left hand. The capture of the left hand is done by drawing a clockwise loop with the right end of the rope over, then under the attacker's arm (Figure 45). At the end of this wraparound motion, deliver a right uppercut to the solar plexus (Figure 46). The delivery of the uppercut completes the loop around his left hand. At this point, your right hand is in a perfect position to drag the attacker down. Grasp the middle of the rope that now encircles both of the attacker's hands and pull down with a jerk (Figure 47). To lend power to the takedown, bend your knees. This puts the greater part of your weight on the attacker's captured hands. At the end of this takedown technique, the attacker's face will hit the ground.

Figure 42

Figure 43

Figure 44

Figure 45

Figure 46

Figure 47

Three

Capturing the attacker's hand presents difficulties, but capturing his kicking leg is even more difficult. Therefore, if the attacker throws a kick, you should attempt to capture a secondary target.

The natural action after a kick is to retract the leg. To capture the leg, you would have to bend low and reach in. However, this will bring your head too close to the attacker—you can end up being pummeled by both of his fists.

The kicker will also normally keep his arms close to his body to keep his balance or to prepare for a punch. There is, however, another type of kicker who spreads his arms out. With the hands close to the body, you would have to reach *in* to capture them. With the hands outstretched, you would have to reach *out* for them. Hence, attempting to capture the hands is not only dangerous but impractical. Aim to capture the head instead.

Capturing the head cannot be accomplished at the instant the kick is delivered. You need to stun the attacker by hitting the kicking leg at the same time that you close the distance. An uppercut delivered simultaneously with your advance will cause the attacker to lower his head. This will give you the chance to capture the head in a loop or in a clothesline.

In Figures 48 and 49, step inside the attacker's roundhouse kick and strike his thigh with your left arm, simultaneously delivering a right uppercut. Form the clockwise loop with the left end of the rope (Figure 50), complete the capture (Figure 51), and strangle the attacker (Figure 52).

Figure 48

Figure 49

Figure 50

Figure 51

Figure 52

Four

Sometimes it is necessary, due to obstructions or to the angle of the kick, to advance toward the attacker on the outside of his kicking leg. This has the additional merit of putting you out of reach of his left hand. In Figure 53, since the attacker's elbow is fully bent, it would be impractical to try to capture it. Thus, the capture must be made on the neck.

Your initial action is to step away from the line of his front kick. At the same time, hit his thigh with a backfist (Figure 54). The blow to the thigh will break his balance and shock him long enough for you to follow up with a right uppercut to the stomach (Figure 55). This will further stun your opponent and will cause him to double up. As he doubles up, graze his forehead with your forearm, bring your right hand over his head, then capture his neck (Figure 56).

This capture is different from a basic loop—it is called a *clothesline* and it is lethal. The rope will hit the attacker's Adam's apple. To lessen the pressure on his throat, the attacker will let himself fall to the ground, butt first (Figure 57). His coccyx will hit the ground, followed by the back of his head.

Figure 53

Figure 54

Figure 55

Figure 56

Figure 57

Five

Capturing the arm with a loop is more difficult when the attacker is holding a knife. Because of the additional length, you would need to reach in with the end of the rope to capture the weapon hand. This reaching in will bring your body dangerously close to the attacker and will result in a cut to your arm. Hence, rather than struggle with looping the arm, avoid it. Instead, capture the neck.

The knife is a very dangerous weapon. You therefore must act quickly to bring the confrontation to an end. Your initial action must be to neutralize the attacker's knife hand.

In Figure 58, as the attacker slashes, hit his forearm powerfully as you simultaneously step in with your right foot. Your advance will bring his face close enough for a right backfist. At the same time, deliver a left uppercut to the solar plexus (Figure 59). The strike to the solar plexus accomplishes two things: It causes the attacker to double up, and it obstructs his knife from making another cut.

Bring the right end of the rope over the attacker's head (Figure 60). As he doubles up and lowers his head, capture it by drawing a clockwise loop with the right end of the rope (Figure 61). At the end of this clockwise loop, take up the slack by stretching your arm and step back with your left foot to bring the attacker down (Figure 62).

Figure 58

Figure 59

Figure 60

Figure 61

Figure 62

Six

Sometimes a clothesline rather than the completion of a loop will be the easier way to make a capture. For example: you hit the attacker in the face and he does not buckle down. Instead, his head tilts backward. If you are taller than the attacker, you can still complete the loop fairly easily. However, a shorter defender will find this difficult and must compensate for his lack of height by using another method of capture—the clothesline.

As the attacker thrusts (Figure 63), sidestep to the right, out of the path of his knife while simultaneously hitting his forearm (Figure 64). Do not allow the attacker to recover from the shock of your initial blow.

Follow up immediately with two simultaneous strikes—one to the left side of his face with your right palmheel and one to the base of his right ear with your left palmheel (Figure 65). While his ear is still ringing, step in with your left foot to the back of your right foot and transfer the left end of the rope to your right hand (Figures 66, 67). Note that it looks as if the attacker will be able to thrust a second time. This is not likely because of the shock of the palmheel strikes you delivered to both sides of his face. You can also guard against this possibility with your left hand.

Step back with your right foot, followed by the bending of your knee, which will transfer your weight to the attacker's throat (Figure 68). The rope will hit his Adam's apple, causing him to become speechless and motionless. This takedown can be lethal.

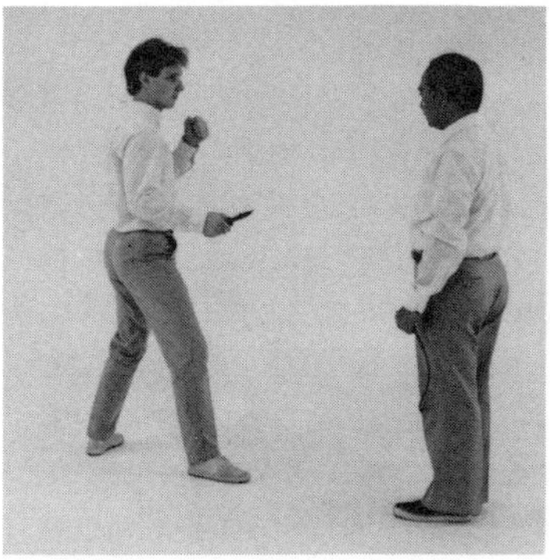

Figure 63

Figure 64

Figure 65

Figure 66

Figure 67

Figure 68

Seven

A slash at the upper right section of your body is best countered by moving toward your left. This takes you away from the reach of the attacker's left hand, brings you to the outside of his attacking arm, and puts you on the attacker's blind side. The quicker you can move in and the closer you can get, the more you can restrict the attacker's knife slash. It is easier to ward off a knife slash when it has just begun than when it has reached its maximum power. This maximum-power point is reached when the attacker's elbow is fully straightened.

You must not let up on your defense. As long as you keep contact with the attacker, you will be able to limit his movements. You *must* maintain contact with the attacker's knife hand at all times. *Do not use power against power.* Rather, feel where the attacker's movements are directed. Your ability to sense his movements will enable you to direct his knife away from your body.

Focus your eye on the attacker's chest (Figure 69). As he attempts to slash, step to your left and hit his elbow with a right hammer-fist (Figure 70). While maintaining contact (with your right hand) with his knife hand, step in with your right foot and deliver a left uppercut to his side (Figure 71). This punch will cause him to bend sideways. As he bends, bring the right end of the rope over his head and capture his neck with a clothesline (Figure 72). Pull hard on both ends of the rope (Figure 73).

Figure 69

Figure 70

Figure 71

Figure 72

Figure 73

Eight

The following method of capture illustrates not only taking advantage of the attacker's momentum but also adding your momentum to his. This approach will allow the smaller or the physically weaker defender to subdue a bigger or stronger attacker.

As the attacker slashes downward (Figure 74), sidestep to your left and block his arm with your right arm (Figure 75). This sidestep will cause the attacker to both hit air and lower his body. Hook his arm with your right hand and push downward to help his momentum along. At the same time, step in with your left foot and turn your body (Figure 76). As his momentum brings him down, slam him at the back of his neck with your left hand (Figure 77). This will cause his knee to hit the ground, possibly breaking his kneecap.

The lowered head puts him in a bad position. On the other hand, this is the best possible position for your capture. Bring the right end of the rope under, then over the attacker's head (Figure 78). Capture his neck by drawing a clockwise loop with the right end of the rope (Figure 79). Tighten the loop to subdue the attacker (Figure 80). If he attempts to stand up, smash his spinal column with your left elbow.

Figure 74

Figure 75

Figure 76

Figure 77

Figure 78

Figure 79

Figure 80

Nine

Your degree of training and your physical makeup place a limit on the power of your technique. For example, look at Figures 81 through 86. The normal method of countering a downward vertical attack is with an upward block to protect the head. However, this can only work if you are physically stronger than your attacker. It is easier to avoid the attack by quickly stepping to the side.

A very effective method of capturing the neck is to throw the rope over the attacker's head. The completion of this maneuver is enhanced if the attacker's momentum is such that he can't stop his forward motion. An example of this situation would be when an attacker slashes forcefully downward. If he has put a lot of power into his attack, his momentum will carry him forward and downward. You, the defender, can take advantage of this to capture his neck rather easily.

As the attacker slashes downward (Figure 81), step forward with your right foot toward his right side (Figure 82). At the same time, graze his arm with your forearm to guide his momentum downward. Throw the rope over his head (Figure 83). Bring your right arm around his front and capture the neck (Figure 84), then step in with your left foot and complete the clothesline (Figure 85). Pull down hard on the two ends of the rope (Figure 86).

Figure 81

Figure 82

Figure 83

Figure 84

Figure 85

Figure 86

Ten

The meanest type of attacker is the knife user. Give him no quarter. At the first twitch of movement, get out of the way! Spring into action and neutralize his knife hand.

While a slash has to be blocked, a knife thrust can be sidestepped and parried. Do not attempt to disarm the attacker, especially if he is bigger than you are. You will have to use agility in order to subdue him. After you make the initial contact with his knife hand, maintain it so you can sense his next action.

If he thrusts at your stomach (Figure 87), sidestep to your left. This will bring you to his blind side, away from a possible punch or kick. At the same time, hit his forearm with your right forearm (Figure 88). Step in with your right foot and hit the attacker by smashing your right hand to his mouth and your left hand to the base of his right ear (Figure 89). While his right ear is still ringing, transfer the right end of the rope to your left hand (Figure 90). Step in with your left foot, then pull on the clothesline (Figure 91). Control his knife hand by keeping it trapped under your armpit. At this time, you can step back with your right foot to drop the attacker on his spinal column.

Figure 87

Figure 88

Figure 89

Figure 90

Figure 91

Eleven

The length of the rope will determine not only the ease or the difficulty of the capture, but also the speed at which the attacker can be subdued. For example, if you are caught in a position where you are holding the two ends of a rope in one hand, you will have only half the length of the rope to work with. The reduced length of the rope, however, has its advantages.

The half rope can be whipped around the attacker's neck. Because it is short, its free end can be easily grabbed. Once grabbed, the takedown can be made quickly. There is practically no slack to the rope. Hence, pulling on it will bring the attacker down fast. The jerk down will be devastating.

As the attacker aims at the right side of your face (Figure 92), step to the left and hit his forearm with your open left hand (Figure 93). Slam the attacker across the face with your right forearm to further stun him (Figure 94). This strike will cause the free end of the rope to whip around the attacker's neck. Grasp the free end with your left hand (Figure 95), tighten the clothesline, and pull (Figure 96).

Figure 92

Figure 93

Figure 94

Figure 95

Figure 96

Twelve

It is also possible to release one end of the rope and make it whip around the attacker's neck. You need not grasp the end of the rope—you only need to grasp the length of the rope closest to your left hand. When grasped in this manner, there will be little slack on the rope and the takedown will be fast and lethal.

Holding the two ends of the rope in your right hand, concentrate your eye on the attacker's chest (Figure 97). As the attacker slashes at your upper right, step in to your left and hit his elbow with your open left hand (Figure 98). Slam the attacker's mouth with your wrist. At the same time, release one end of the rope. This will cause the free end of the rope to whip around the attacker's neck (Figure 99). Make sure that you keep control over the attacker's knife hand (with your left hand) to prevent him from slashing again. Push the attacker's elbow, grasp the length of the rope with your left hand, tighten the loop, and pull the attacker down (Figure 100).

Figure 97

Figure 98

Figure 99

Figure 100

Thirteen

The knife is a lethal weapon, so you must not lose sight of it for an instant. Do not look directly at it; keep it inside your peripheral vision. Fear could very well enter your mind. Hence, you must train to concentrate on the attacker. One of his shirt buttons is a good spot to focus on. This will block out the glint of his blade.

The completion of a clockwise loop, a counterclockwise loop, or a clothesline is necessary but time-consuming. Thus, if you can save the time to complete the loop or the clothesline, you can put the time saved to good use. You can subdue the attacker more quickly if you are able to hold the rope with a loop already formed (Figure 101).

As the attacker slashes at your upper left, step in to the right (Figure 102). Simultaneously, hit his forearm with your left palmheel. Close the distance by stepping in with your left foot (Figure 103). At the same time, throw the loop over his head. In one motion, you have completed a capture very quickly. Step in with your right foot toward his back, bend your knee, and pull the loop with your right hand to bring the attacker down on his back (Figure 104).

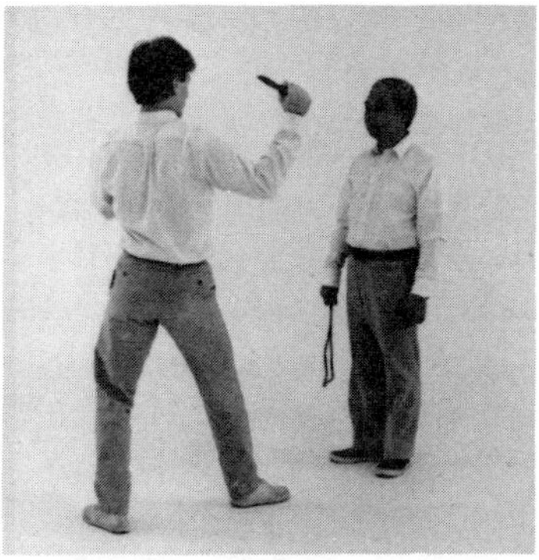

Figure 101

Figure 102

Figure 103

Figure 104

Fourteen

Capturing the arm by drawing a loop around it is impossible when the opponent is holding a stick because the length of the stick will hinder the completion of the loop.

You can still complete a capture in one of two ways. First, simultaneous with striking the forearm, you can release one end of the rope and throw it over the forearm. Second, instead of throwing one end of the rope over, you can hit the attacker a second time—this will bring the two ends of the rope close together. At this time, you may transfer one end of the rope to the other hand. Having the ends of the rope in the grasp of one hand completes a loop and the capture.

You *must* take the attacker down—he will not go willingly. Therefore, you need to hit him one more time—with your right hand (which is closest to him) on the crook of his elbow. After the strike, retract your right hand and hit the opponent's wrist with it, then pull with both your right hand and with the loop in your left hand.

Focus your eye on the attacker's chest (Figure 105). Sidestep the stick attack and hit his forearm (Figure 106). Hit the attacker's arm with your left hand and transfer the right end of the rope to your left hand (Figure 107). Then, strike the attacker's neck with the back of your open hand (Figure 108). Push down on the attacker's shoulder with your right hand. At the same time, pull the loop to bring the attacker down on his back (Figure 109).

Figure 105

Figure 106

Figure 107

Figure 108

Figure 109

Fifteen

It is critical that you act quickly when an attacker swings a stick at you. Move in! If you maintain a stick-length distance from him, you will be at a disadvantage. The closer you can get to the attacker, the more you will be able to restrict the movements of his stick.

It is easier to ward off a stick strike at its inception than when it has reached its full power. Hence, it is necessary for you to get close quickly. Once you are close, you can feel the direction of his next attack. Don't give him another chance to strike. Do not let up on your offense. Each of your strikes should set up the attacker for the rope capture.

In Figure 110, the attacker aims a strike at your upper right. Step toward your left and hit his elbow with your right hand (Figure 111). Step in with your right foot and deliver a left uppercut to the side (Figure 112). This punch will cause him to buckle up (Figure 113). At this point the two ends of the rope are not yet close enough to make a capture. With your right hand, punch the attacker a third time in the chest (Figure 114). This will further stun him and will also bring the two ends of the rope close together. Transfer the right end of the rope to your left hand to capture the attacker's right hand. Pull down on the loop. At the same time, smash the attacker in the face with your right hand (Figure 115).

Figure 110

Figure 111

Figure 112

Figure 113

Figure 114

Figure 115

Sixteen

It is always best to stop an attack at its inception. However, the attacker who is set on trouble almost always makes the first move, catching his intended victims by surprise. You will therefore have to strive for equality after the attacker's initial action. This is like chess, where white always has the first move. The strategy for the player with the black pieces is to first gain equality. Once he achieves equality, then, and only then, does he aim for a win.

In Figure 116, the attacker has the better position, since he is at least a stick length away. As he thrusts, step to the outside of his weapon arm. At the same time, hit his fist (Figure 117). At this time, you have achieved equality—you can neutralize any move he tries to make. You have really gained the upper hand because his movements are restricted. The only way he can use the stick again is to draw it back. Do not let him.

Deliver a quick right uppercut to the solar plexus (Figure 118). This uppercut will in itself end the fight if delivered with enough power. However, make no such assumption. Deliver a left uppercut to his side (Figure 119), which will bring the two ends of the rope together. Transfer the right end of the rope to your left hand (Figure 120). Jerk on the loop to bring the attacker down (Figure 121).

Figure 116

Figure 117

Figure 118

Figure 119

Figure 120

Figure 121

Seventeen

A folded chain can also be used to capture an attacker's neck. Because it is short, you need to advance quickly to make the capture. This advance must be disguised with a blow to the attacker's weapon arm. These principles are illustrated in Figures 122 through 126.

Concentrate on an object on the attacker's chest (Figure 122). As the knife slash approaches your upper right, step in to your left with your left foot. At the same time, hit the attacker's elbow with your right hand (Figure 123). Hit the attacker's elbow a second time with your open left hand. This strike will position the chain for maximum whipping effect (Figure 124). Smash the attacker's jaw with your right forearm. This strike accomplishes two things: it further stuns the attacker and whips the chain around his neck (Figure 125). Grasp the free end of the chain with your left hand, tighten the loop, and subdue the attacker (Figure 126).

It is hoped that the strikes used in this defense will break the attacker's elbow. However, the attacker can still kick. Hence, you need to take him down. There is nothing more effective than a takedown to complete the domination of an attacker.

Figure 122

Figure 123

Figure 124

Figure 125

Figure 126

Eighteen

You can also club an attacker into submission with a chain. To accomplish this, you will need to get close enough to hit him without getting hit by his first attack.

In Figure 127, the attacker aims a knife thrust at your belly. Sidestep to the left, parry the thrust with your open left hand, and twist your body to the side (Figure 128). This twist will allow your body to coil for your follow-up attack. Hit the attacker across the face with the chain (Figure 129). Keep contact with his knife hand so you can feel the direction of his next possible attack. The blow to the attacker's face will whip the chain around his neck. Step up with your right foot (Figure 130), grasp the free end of the chain with your left hand, and complete the capture of the neck. Tighten the loop and make him drop his knife. If he does not, jerk the chain down (Figure 131).

A powerful blow in Figure 129 can knock the attacker out. However, a knife user is a very dangerous adversary. Proceed with your counters on the assumption that he will still be able to thrust with his weapon. Keeping contact with the attacker's arm or body will warn you of the slightest twitch of his muscles. This will allow you to stop his every move until he is completely subdued.

Figure 127

Figure 128

Figure 129

Figure 130

Figure 131

Nineteen

The chain is a versatile weapon. You can club an attacker with it or you can capture his neck, arm, or leg. Because of its weight and its strength, you can subdue an attacker simply by striking him.

You can grip the chain with both ends in one hand. Held in this manner, your accuracy will be enhanced and you need not take up any slack. This will make your strike reach the target faster and will also result in powerful blows.

As the attacker aims a slash at the right side of your face (Figure 132), step to the left with your left foot and hit his forearm with a left palmheel (Figure 133). This will break the momentum of his attack. Also, your body twist will position your chain for maximum whipping effect. While keeping control of his knife hand with your left hand, hit the attacker across the face with the chain (Figure 134). This will stun him and will allow you to step in with your right foot. Note that this forward step can become a kick to the shin. Finish off the attacker by pulling his right shoulder with your left hand and pushing his head down with your right fist (Figure 135).

Figure 132

Figure 133

Figure 134

Figure 135

Twenty

You can also use the full length of a chain when defending yourself. Although you need better skill in order to hit the attacker from a longer range, the distance will allow you to strike him without getting hit yourself.

By holding one end of the chain, you can maintain a safe distance—a distance not available when you hold both ends in one hand. To effect a capture, however, you will need to step in and attack a second time. These principles are illustrated in Figures 136 through 141.

As the stick approaches your upper left (Figure 136), whip the attacker's fist with the chain (Figure 137). This will either make the attacker recoil or will make him motionless (Figure 138). Hit the attacker a second time on his back (Figure 139). This will further stun him and will allow you to close the distance safely (Figure 140). Grasp the free end of the chain with your left hand, then capture his neck by drawing a counterclockwise loop with the right end of the chain (Figure 141). Tighten the loop to subdue the attacker.

Figure 136

Figure 137

Figure 138

Figure 139

Figure 140

Figure 141

Twenty-one

While a rope can be used to strike an attacker, its sting is less than that of a chain. If done powerfully enough, a blow from a chain will discourage or completely stop an attacker.

The attacker moves in with a stick (Figure 142). It is very important that you make initial contact with your chain as he strikes (Figure 143). This will break his concentration and will prevent him from executing a second attack. As he recoils from the blow, step in with your right foot and hit his fist a second time with the chain (Figures 144, 145). Close the distance further by leaning forward and grab the weapon arm. This grab immobilizes the weapon arm (Figure 146) and will allow the final blow that can finish the attacker off (Figure 147).

Your initial strike with the chain must be accompanied by a step back to avoid getting hit by the attacker's long stick. This retreat is necessary because you only have half a chain to fight with at the outset. The distance of your step must be just enough to avoid getting hit and to allow you to step back in to reach your target.

Figure 142

Figure 143

Figure 144

Figure 145

Figure 146

Figure 147

Rope: Defense Against Grabs and Holds

In a self-defense situation, you must always keep a safe distance between you and the attacker. However, this safe distance can be breached. The attacker, by some premeditated surprise move, might be able to grab your hand or your collar. Of greater danger is a bear hug or a choke hold from behind. The greatest danger is presented when the attacker is able to grab you with one hand and threatens you with a knife in the other. These are critical situations, so you do not have any time to lose. The situation calls for quick thinking and action.

You are in the greatest danger if a knife is pressed against your body. Your primary concern is to direct the point away. Having redirected the point of the knife, you must maintain control over the attacker's knife hand to prevent him from initiating a thrust or a slash. Your next concern is to force him to loosen or to release his hold.

Because of the need for quick counters, you must be able to use all parts of your body as weapons. You can use your forehead or the back of your head in a headbutt to the attacker's face. You can also use your butt to hit the attacker's groin.

After making the initial strike, the methods of escape are many and varied. They follow certain patterns and principles. These are:

1. A blow to the attacker's body or on the grabbing arm to break or at least loosen the hold.
2. Displacement of your body to minimize or eliminate the possibility of getting cut.
3. A quick follow-up blow to the body or to the arm to further stun the attacker.
4. The application of capture techniques.
5. The takedown to subdue the attacker.

One

The attacker has breached your first line of defense—distance—by seizing your shirt with both hands (Figure 148). However, all is not lost. While he has you in a hold, he cannot strike you (though he can push or pull you to take you down).

Hit the attacker with a right uppercut to the solar plexus. At the same time, bring the left end of the rope over his right hand and press with it (Figure 149). Losing no time, hit the attacker on his forearm with your right forearm. This accomplishes two things: it further stuns the attacker and brings the two ends of the rope close together (Figure 150). Transfer the right end of the rope to your left hand, then press down on his elbow, putting the weight of your shoulder on his arm (Figure 151).

You are too close to the attacker to be able to punch him, and you are bent too low to kick him. You can, however, do one of two things: you can smash him on the side of his face with your forehead, or you can nudge him with your shoulder (Figure 152). The nudge will cause him to fall (Figure 153). Once on the ground, he will be at your mercy.

Figure 148

Figure 149

Figure 150

Figure 151

Figure 152

Figure 153

Two

The attacker has grabbed you by your throat. You can either move back or stand your ground, but both reactions can have unpleasant results. If you move back, you will encourage more of an attack. Also, you would have to move back in to hit the attacker, giving him time to defend himself.

At the first sign that you are resisting, the attacker can take a swipe at you with his left hand (Figure 154). Do not resist. Relax, then move!

Step to the outside of his right foot with your left foot. At the same time, hit his arm down with your left hand (Figure 155). Follow up immediately with a right uppercut to the solar plexus (Figure 156). Timed properly and applied powerfully, the uppercut should end the confrontation. However, never make the assumption that the attacker has no more fight left in him.

Smash the bridge of his nose with your forearm. This will make him close his eyes instinctively and therefore make him oblivious to the rope capture. Bring the right end of the rope up and over his head (Figure 157). Draw a counterclockwise loop to capture his neck (Figure 158). Because of the position of his arm, the right end of the rope might not get to his throat. However, the left length of the rope is cutting at it. This will be enough to bring him down (Figure 159).

Figure 154

Figure 155

Figure 156

Figure 157

Figure 158

Figure 159

Three

The attacker has grabbed your hand (Figure 160). Chances are he will pull hard, kick with his right foot, or punch with his right hand. The first sign that you are tensing your arm will cause him to react, so relax.

Step in with your right foot toward your right. This will take you away from a possible kick or punch. Remember not to tense or move your arm from where he is holding it. This initial nonresistance will throw him off until you are ready to attack. Punch to the chest (Figure 161). At the same time, begin the capture of his arm (Figure 162). Rotate your right fist under, then over the attacker's forearm. At the end of this rotation, grasp the other length of the rope with your right hand (Figure 163). Take up the slack by pulling with your left hand. At the same time, pull with your right hand as it completes the loop (Figure 164).

The success of your initial blow—the punch to the chest—will depend upon complete relaxation. You must train to make your hand limp after the attacker grabs you. The success of the takedown, on the other hand, depends upon properly bending your knee. Note that while the outward appearance is the simple bending of the knee, the real purpose of the bend is to put the weight of your body on the attacker's wrist.

Figure 160

Figure 161

Figure 162

Figure 163

Figure 164

Four

You have allowed yourself to be caught unaware. The man trying to choke you might be a prankster, a friend, or a real attacker set on causing harm. There is no time to find out which one he is.

Tuck in your chin to prevent the attacker's forearm from reaching your throat (Figure 165). Immediately, hit his groin with your butt. At the same time, press on his choking arm with your left hand (Figure 166). Retaining a hold on the wrist of the choking hand, step back with your left foot. Note that this step can be a hook on the attacker's right ankle. At the same time that you step back, lower your head and move it toward the opening of his bent arm (Figure 167). Twist the attacker's arm. As soon as you get your head free (Figure 168), bring the right end of the rope over his head. Take up the slack to capture his neck in a clothesline, then yank down hard (Figures 169, 170).

The key to your escape is the tucking in of your chin. If you fail in this, none of the subsequent techniques can be executed. As an aid to the instinctive tucking in of the chin, exercise (alone) by moving your chin up and down. A few minutes a day with this exercise will enable you to tuck in your chin automatically if the need arises.

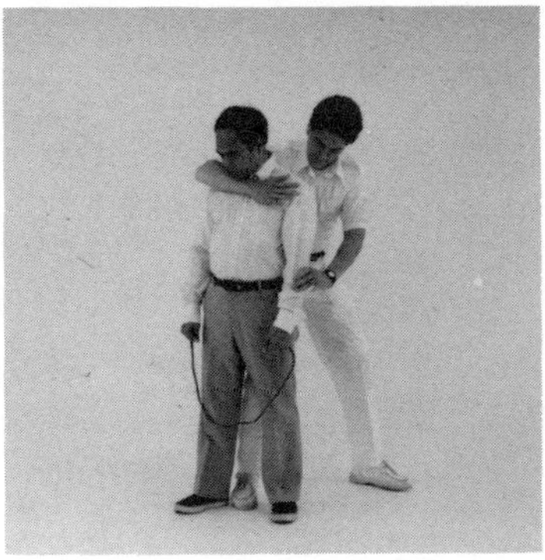

Figure 165

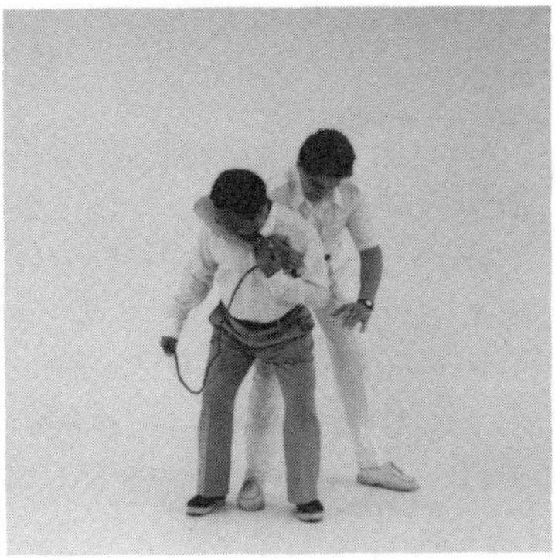

Figure 166

Figure 167

Figure 168

Figure 169

Figure 170

Five

Though the situation in Figures 171 through 176 might easily be a friendly hand over your shoulder, it might not be so. The attacker has not struck you, but he can—soon.

Relax. Do not look at the attacker. Keep your eyes front, then move (Figure 171).

Hit the attacker's stomach with a left-hand back-fist (Figure 172). Follow up to the same spot with a right uppercut (Figure 173). These two quick punches to the same spot will make the attacker double up and will cause him to lower his head. Strike his eyes with your forearm (Figure 174). This blow to the eyes will bring the right end of the rope above his head. Draw a counterclockwise loop with the right end of the rope over, then under the attacker's head (Figure 175). Take up the slack and tighten the loop around his neck (Figure 176).

A hand on the shoulder looks harmless. This innocent-looking hold, however, can deteriorate to your disadvantage. Hence, there is a need for you to counter it. If the hold turns out to be a prank, you can apologize later. Should it turn out to be a real threat, then you have saved yourself a lot of harm.

Figure 171

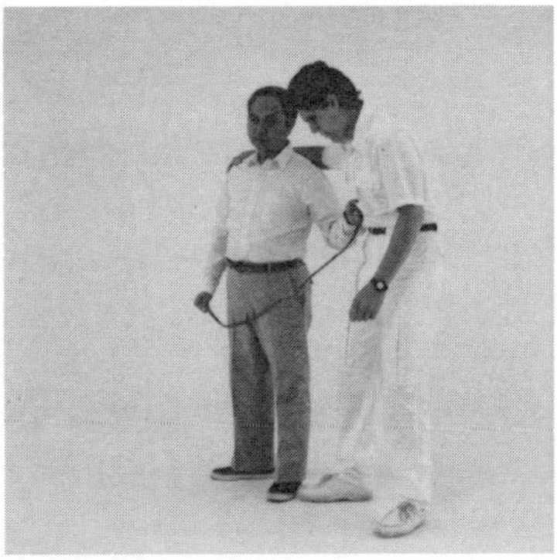

Figure 172

Figure 173

Figure 174

Figure 175

Figure 176

Six

The attacker has pinned both your hands to your sides with a bear hug (Figure 177). He cannot strike at you from this position, but he can wrestle or throw you down. Offer no resistance, then spring into action!

Smash the attacker in the face with the back of your head (Figure 178). This will cause him to loosen his hold a bit. Follow up quickly by hitting his groin with your butt. This will cause him to lean away and release his hold (Figure 179). Without any hesitation, throw the rope over your head to capture the attacker's head (Figure 180). Bend your knee and escape from under his left hand. Step back with your right foot (Figure 181), then jerk on the two ends of the rope to strangle him (Figure 182). This step back can be a hook on the attacker's left foot, as well.

The key to the success of your counters is the initial headbutt and the groin strike with your butt. If you slam the attacker hard enough with your head, there may be no need to capture his neck. The strike to the groin is both painful and surprising. After you tighten the loop, tighten it further or jerk it down at the slightest twitch of the attacker's muscles.

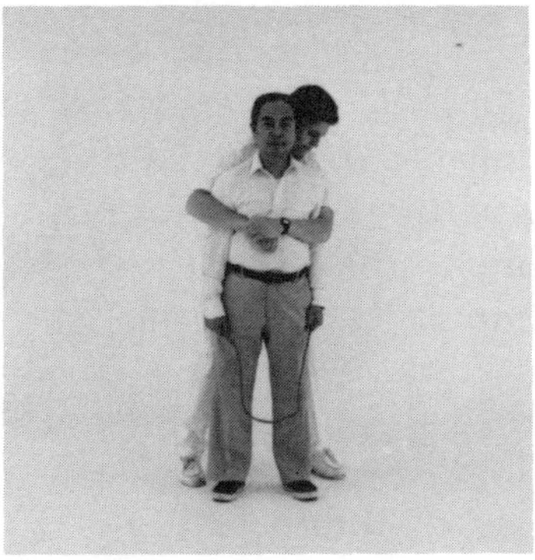

Figure 177

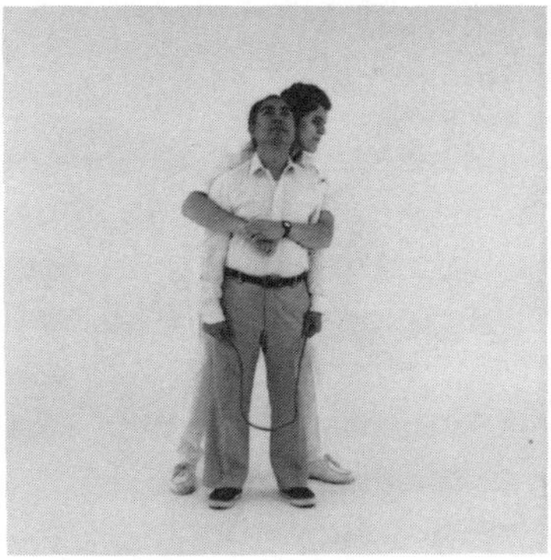

Figure 178

Figure 179

Figure 180

Figure 181

Figure 182

Seven

The attacker puts a knife against your throat (Figure 183). You can do one of two things: step back and run, or stay and fight. Running might not be the best way to get out of this jam, however. He may run after you. Hence, you should conserve your energy and stand your ground. You either fight now or fight later.

Your first concern is to direct the knife away from your throat. Having done this, you will have to *keep* it away. You need to act quickly.

Turn your head to the right while simultaneously hitting the attacker's knife hand away from your throat with your left hand (Figure 184). Having gotten rid of the threatening point, you have more freedom of movement. Maintain control over his knife hand with your left hand and deliver a right uppercut to the solar plexus (Figure 185). This punch, both shocking and painful, will cause the attacker to double up and lower his head.

Bring the right end of the rope over the attacker's head (Figure 186). Complete the counterclockwise loop for the capture (Figure 187). You will notice that the attacker's knife hand was also captured by the rope, making this move even more potent. If you tighten the loop, the knife might even hit his throat or face.

Figure 183

Figure 184

Figure 185

Figure 186

Figure 187

Eight

The attacker has grabbed you and has aimed a knife at your face (Figure 188). This is a life-threatening situation. You do not have any alternative but to fight back.

Keep your eyes on an object on the attacker's chest, such as a button. As he thrusts with the knife, step in toward his back with your right foot. At the same time, block his knife hand with your left forearm, close to the elbow (Figure 189). At this point, deliver a right uppercut to the solar plexus. As he doubles up, strike his mouth with your forearm (Figure 190). This will bring up the left end of the rope (it can also knock him down). Having stunned the attacker, capture his neck in a clothesline. Finish him off with a right hammerfist on the spinal column (Figure 191).

The key to the successful completion of these techniques is the near simultaneous strikes of the right uppercut to the solar plexus and the block at the attacker's knife arm. Totally absorbed with his knife thrust and with the advantage he has, the attacker may become oblivious to your right uppercut until it's too late. This blow will be a shock to him and can very well finish the fight.

Figure 188

Figure 189

Figure 190

Figure 191

Nine

The attacker has you in a very dangerous predicament. He has you by the neck with his left arm and is threatening you with the point of his knife pressed against your side (Figure 192).

First things first! Smash the attacker's groin with your right hand (Figure 193). At the same time, press hard on the choking hand with your left hand. The strike to the groin will be very painful and will stun the attacker. It will make him recoil, pushing the threatening point away from your body, and will allow you to bring the left end of the rope over his head (Figure 194). Take up the slack on the rope by jerking at both ends (Figure 195). You can also knee the attacker in the face.

Do not make the mistake of first trying to pry loose the hand choke. The knife poses the greater danger. You *must* direct it away from your body with your very first move.

Figure 192

Figure 193

Figure 194

Figure 195

Ten

The attacker has you in a left-hand choke. Much more dangerous, however, is the knife he has on your throat (Figure 196). Relax. Offer no resistance. Then move!

Your first concern is to direct the knife away from your throat. You can't afford to miss on your first try! Simultaneously, twist your body to the right, push the knife away from your throat with your left hand, and hit the attacker's groin with your right hand (Figure 197). Quickly slip from under his choking arm while maintaining your grip on the wrist of his knife hand (Figure 198). Step back with your right leg, hooking his left leg in the process (Figure 199). The hook will cause the attacker's leg to spread out.

Slam the attacker on the back of his head with the crook of your elbow. This will bring the right end of the rope over his head (Figure 200). Draw a counter-clockwise loop over, then under the attacker's head to capture his neck (Figure 201). At this point, you can elbow him on the spinal column. Putting your whole weight behind the elbow would result in a lethal takedown.

Figure 196

Figure 197

Figure 198

Figure 199

Figure 200

Figure 201

Belt and Necktie: Defense Against Empty-Hand Attacks

A belt is especially suited for self-defense for several reasons: it is sturdy, it is provided with a buckle, and it is commonly worn around the waist. The use of the belt, however, puts you at least two moves behind the attacker. First, you have to open up the buckle; second, you have to pull it out. Similarly, a necktie puts you two moves behind. First, you have to unloop it; second, you have to take it off your neck before you can use it.

A smooth belt is ideally suited for a quick pull and release. As you pull the belt out, make sure that there is minimum whipping effect. The whipping effect will slow down your release, which in turn will reduce the speed of your counters. The noisier your pullout, the slower your counter will be. For the quickest release, pull your belt out at a tangent with your waistline. Practice this move using your right, and then do so with the left.

You must have one hand free during the pullout. This will allow you to defend against the first attack. At the same time that you parry, you must complete the release of your belt or the unlooping of your tie. At the completion of the release or unlooping, your fist must make contact with the attacker's body. If you are able to pull the belt out or unloop the tie quickly, the attacker's initial advantage will be gone.

A series of strikes is necessary before you can complete the loop. This will allow you to close the distance and to properly position the two ends of the belt or tie to complete the capture of the arm, neck, or leg.

The belt used in the photographs is 40½ inches long and 1$\frac{3}{16}$ inches wide. The buckle is worn at the left side. The tie is 57 inches long.

One

A common form of attack is a right-hand slap to the face (Figure 202). Unbuckle your belt and grasp the buckle in your right hand. As the slap approaches, step to your right and block the attacker's arm with your left knife hand (Figure 203). This initial block is very important. If you miss, you will not have time to pull out your belt. The block will also shock him long enough to prevent him from punching with his left hand.

Pull out your belt. At the end of the pull-out movement, deliver a right uppercut to his stomach (Figure 204). This will cause him to double up. Graze his jaw with your right elbow (Figure 205). This will bring the buckle close to your left hand. Transfer the buckle to your left hand, grasp the length of the belt, then hit the attacker on the side of his neck with the back of your open right hand (Figure 206). Finish him off by grabbing his wrist with your right hand, stepping back, and pulling down hard with your left hand on the completed loop (Figure 207). Note that the step back will clear your knee away from the attacker's head at the same time that you put your body weight on his wrist.

Figure 202

Figure 203

Figure 204

Figure 205

Figure 206

Figure 207

Two

The attacker aims a backhand slap at your face (Figure 208). Talk to him—try to calm him down. At the same time, however, unbuckle your belt and grasp the buckle with your right hand. Attempting to reason with him will distract his attention away from your hands.

As he attacks, step to the left with your left foot and hit his elbow with your left palmheel (Figure 209). Note that this movement results in a body twist. This twist will facilitate the release of your belt. Kick the attacker's shin with your right foot, then stomp on his foot. At the same time, pull out your belt (Figure 210).

Push the attacker's right elbow with your left hand and strike across his face with the belt (Figure 211). This will cause the free end of the belt to whip around his neck. Grasp the free end with your left hand. You have now caught the attacker's neck in a loop. Tighten the loop by pulling down hard with both hands at the same time that you step toward his back with your right foot (Figure 212).

Figure 208

Figure 209

Figure 210

Figure 211

Figure 212

Three

The attacker aims a right-hand punch at your solar plexus. Keep calm. Try to talk him out of it. At the same time, while he is trying to figure out what you are saying, unbuckle your belt and grasp the buckle with your right hand (Figure 213).

As he punches, step to the outside of his arm and hit his elbow with a left-hand palmheel (Figure 214). At the same time, twist your body and pull your belt out with your right hand. At the end of the release, deliver a right uppercut to his stomach (Figure 215). Make sure you put your body weight behind the uppercut. The attacker will double up. Quickly bring the buckle down and around his right leg (Figure 216) and transfer the buckle to your left hand (Figure 217). Pull his legs apart by jerking on the belt with your left hand (Figure 218).

The key to the success of this takedown is the power behind the uppercut. If delivered powerfully enough, the punch alone will finish the fight. However, you should add this leg takedown to your repertoire of techniques for some possible future use.

Figure 213

Figure 214

Figure 215

Figure 216

Figure 217

Figure 218

Four

In addition to right-hand pullouts, you should also become proficient with left-hand pullouts. In Figure 219, the attacker aims to slap you. Distract his attention with some ruse. Call out a friend's name at his back. He may not believe you, but it should distract him long enough for you to get your hands on your belt.

As he slaps, step in with your right foot. Make sure you do not advance too closely—he can still punch with his left. At the same time that you take a step forward, hit his forearm with a right knife-hand (Figure 220). This will distract him from kicking or punching. Quickly, deliver two simultaneous strikes: one to his face with a right-hand backfist; the other, to his stomach with a left uppercut (Figure 221). Notice that the belt's release is totally hidden from his view.

Do not let up on your attack. While he has not yet recovered from the pain and shock of the last two strikes, hit the crook of his elbow with your forearm (Figure 222). At this point, you can also smash his cheekbone with your forehead. The strike to the crook of the elbow will bring the buckle close to your right hand. Transfer the buckle to your right hand to complete the capture. Step back (Figure 223), put your body weight on the captured wrist, and pull down hard (Figure 224). This can be a lethal takedown because the attacker will most likely hit the ground head first.

Figure 219

Figure 220

Figure 221

Figure 222

Figure 223

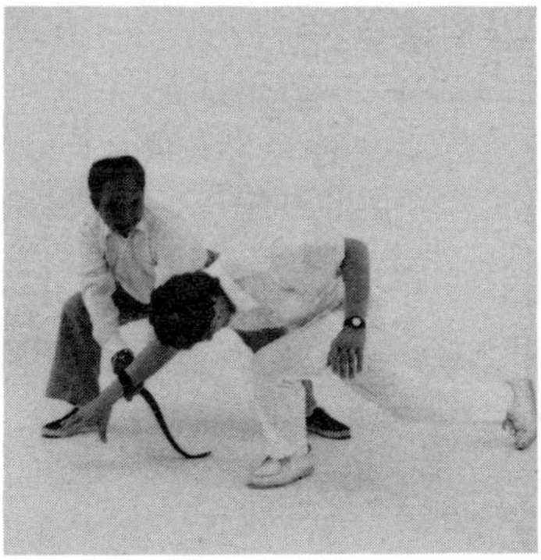

Figure 224

Five

Try to distract the attacker by mumbling words totally foreign to him. He will not understand you, but it will catch his ears. In the meantime, unbuckle your belt and grasp the buckle with your left hand (Figure 225).

As he punches with his right, step to the outside and block his forearm with your right elbow (Figure 226). This block will take his attention away from your next move. Pull out the belt with your left hand while maintaining contact (with your right hand) with his right hand. At the end of the pullout, deliver a left uppercut to his side (Figure 227). Follow up your advantage quickly with a right-hand palmheel to the jaw (Figure 228).

Transfer the buckle to your right hand and complete the loop to capture the arm (Figures 229, 230). Strike his biceps with your right elbow, then pull down (Figure 231). At this time, you can sweep his left foot from under him.

Figure 225

Figure 226

Figure 227

Figure 228

Figure 229

Figure 230

Figure 231

Six

It is not easy to subdue an attacker with a necktie. However, with practice it is possible. The important thing is to distract the attacker with successive attacks until you can unloop the tie and complete a capture.

As the attacker aims a backhand slap at your face, step in to the outside of his arm and block with your right forearm (Figure 232). This will prevent a possible left-hand punch or left-foot kick. Having stunned the attacker, you can further close the distance. Step in with your right foot. At the same time, hit his triceps with your left elbow (Figure 233). This will bring your fists close to the loop of your tie. Grasp the ends of the loop with both hands (Figure 234).

Pull the loop apart. The loop's resistance to being untied will lend power to the backfist that you will smash into the attacker's face (Figure 235). This powerful blow will shock him and will allow you time to bring the right end of the tie above (Figure 236) then around the attacker's neck (Figure 237). Take up the slack on the tie and tighten it (Figure 238). You are now in a perfect position to throw the attacker by jerking down on the ends of the tie or by nudging his right knee with your right knee.

Figure 232

Figure 233

Figure 234

Figure 235

Figure 236

Figure 237

Figure 238

Seven

The attacker takes aim at the left side of your face (Figure 239). Distract him with some ruse. Yell!

As he slaps, step to the right with your right foot (but do not advance too close to his left hand). At the same time that you step forward, block his forearm with your left knife-hand (Figure 240). This will stun him long enough for you to advance and close the distance even more (Figure 241). Maintain contact (with your left hand) with the attacker's hand so you can detect the slightest motion. Slam his chest with your right elbow (Figure 242). This will bring your right fist close to the loop on your tie. Grasp the ends of the loop with both hands.

Pull hard on the loop. The tie will be loosened. Direct your backfist at the attacker's face (Figure 243). The backfist will stun the attacker long enough for you to bring the left end of the tie up, over, then around the attacker's neck (Figure 244). Tighten the loop by jerking hard on both ends of the tie (Figure 245). Note that after the backfist to the face, you can follow up by smashing the attacker's mouth with your forehead.

Figure 239

Figure 240

Figure 241

Figure 242

Figure 243

Figure 244

Figure 245

Rope: Defense Against Firearms

Reaction time is the time it takes a person to respond to a given signal, such as a hand or foot attack. The reaction time of an average person is from one-half to three-quarters of a second. The duration of the reaction time is a most critical aspect of self-defense. The shorter it is for you, the better your chances are of overpowering the opponent.

Reaction time depends upon preparedness, your skill level, and the complexity of the attack. Reaction time may be measured in relative time by the following illustration. Give a partner an unloaded gun. Let him point the gun toward you within your arm's reach. Tell him to pull the trigger at your first motion.

Hit your partner's gun hand at the same time that you twist your body to the side. He will react to your first movement and will attempt to pull the trigger. The time it takes your partner to see your move and pull the trigger is his reaction time. Your move will take your partner by surprise and you will be able to knock the gun aside or even out of his grasp. With practice, you will even have time to spare.

Given these principles of self-defense, you should recognize the need to act quickly when confronted by a man with a gun. If you were able to knock your partner's gun aside in less than half a second, you would have made the most important step in subduing an opponent. Of course, it is very important that you immediately close the distance so you can control the opponent's gun hand after the weapon is pointed away from you.

A person with a gun may not be within your arm's reach. If he is intent on a stickup or a robbery, however, he will need to get close to you to hide the gun from the view of other persons in the vicinity. Furthermore, a person with a gun is always overconfident. He will wave the gun in your face or prod you with it, knowing that he has the power of life and death over you. Hence, he normally will be within arm's reach. If he is not, you must plead, beg, or even get down on your knees to create the opportunity to get near him.

One

The opponent aims a revolver at your chest (Figure 246). You are in a critical situation. Try to reason with him. Then act!

Twist your body to the side and hit the gunman's fist with your left hand, thus directing the gun away from your body. At the same time, step with your left foot to the outside of his gun hand (Figure 247). Quickly deliver a right palmheel to his solar plexus. Do not release the right end of the rope. At the same time, maintain control over the gun hand with your left hand (Figure 248).

You are still in danger because your opponent's finger is still on the trigger. Do not let up on your attack. Graze his eyes with the crook of your right elbow (Figure 249). This will bring the right end of the rope over his head. With the right end of the rope, draw a counterclockwise loop around his neck and take up the slack (Figure 250). Step back with your right foot to further tighten the loop (Figure 251). At this point, you can jerk both ends of the rope to bring him down.

Figure 246

Figure 247

Figure 248

Figure 249

Figure 250

Figure 251

The key to the successful completion of this capture is the initial hit on the opponent's gun hand. Your advance in Figure 247 is disguised by a right palmheel to the solar plexus. Having closed the distance, you still need to stun the opponent further by grazing him on the eyes with the crook of your elbow. Remember to tighten the loop by jerking down with the right end of the rope and simultaneously punching upward with the left end of the rope.

Two

The opponent aims a gun at your head, a very dangerous predicament (Figure 252). Act quickly!

Slant your head to your left and hit the opponent's fist with your right hand, sweeping it toward your upper right. Directly afterward, take a step forward toward the opponent's right side with your left foot (Figure 253). This step will move your head farther away from the gun's line of fire.

Step in deeper toward his back. At the same time, hook the opponent's gun hand by drawing a clockwise circle with your right hand. Then strike him at the back of his neck with your left hand (Figure 254). These two actions will force his head down. The neck strike will stun the opponent and prevent him from re-aiming his gun.

Slam the opponent's nose with your right forearm (Figure 255). This will force his head to tilt backward. Quickly step in and capture his neck with a clothesline and pull on both ends of the rope (Figure 256). This will take up the slack on both ends. At this point the rope will cut into the opponent's neck. He will try to lean on you for support. By stepping away, you can drop him on his back (Figure 257).

You must recognize that multiple strikes are necessary to stun the opponent. At the same time, they will enable you to close the distance and to bring the two ends of the rope progressively closer until you can complete the capture. At the end of each strike, notice the progressive closing of the distance and the two ends of the rope getting closer together.

Figure 252

Figure 253

Figure 254

Figure 255

Figure 256

Figure 257

Three

The opponent presses a gun at your right side behind your right elbow (Figure 258). Relax your body. Then move!

Twist your body clockwise and grab the opponent's gun hand with your right hand. Simultaneously, step back with your right foot to the outside of the gun hand. This backward step and body twist will direct the gun away from your body. At the end of this movement, punch the opponent at the base of his right ear with your left hand (Figure 259). Continue your turn and step deep behind his back with your left foot. At the same time, hook his arm with your right hand and press down on his neck with your left hand (Figure 260). This will force the opponent's head down. At this time, his gun hand will be trapped between your right arm and leg.

Place your left elbow on his back to prevent him from standing up. At the same time, strike his eyes with the crook of your elbow (Figure 261). Bring up the right end of the rope and complete the counterclockwise loop around the opponent's neck. At this time, control his neck by pressing down firmly with your left hand (Figure 262). Pull with the right end of the rope and punch with the left end to subdue the opponent (Figure 263).

The success of these techniques will depend upon your first two movements: the initial body turn and the step back with your right foot. These are critical movements and can only be completed from a totally relaxed position. Any sign of tensing before your movement will alert the opponent to your intentions.

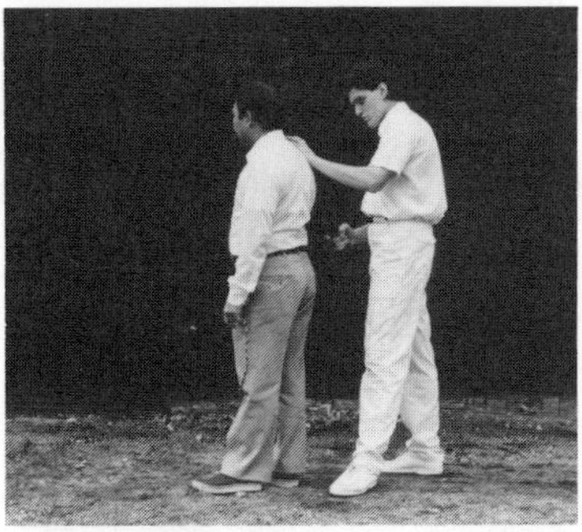

Figure 258

Figure 259

Figure 260

Figure 261

Figure 262

Figure 263

Four

The opponent aims a gun at the back of your head (Figure 264). Do not tense. Relax.

Quickly slant your head away from the gun. Pivoting on your right foot, turn your body clockwise. At the same time, hit the gun hand with your triceps and the right side of the opponent's face with the back of your open right hand (Figure 265). Continue your turn while pivoting on your right foot and step toward the opponent's back with your left foot. At the same time, hook the gun hand with your right hand and grab the back of his neck with your left hand (Figure 266). At this time, his gun hand will be trapped between your right hand and leg.

The opponent will still be full of fight, so do not let him recover from your initial attack. Strike his eyes with your right forearm (Figure 267), remembering to keep the pressure on the back of his neck with your left hand. This eye strike will temporarily blind the opponent and will allow you the time to draw a counterclockwise loop with the right end of the rope (Figure 268). Pull back on the right end of the rope and punch with your left hand (Figure 269). This punch and pull will put tremendous pressure on the opponent's throat.

It is critical in your initial turn (Figure 265) that you forcefully hit the opponent's gun hand. This will surprise him, spoil his aim, and prevent him from re-aiming the gun.

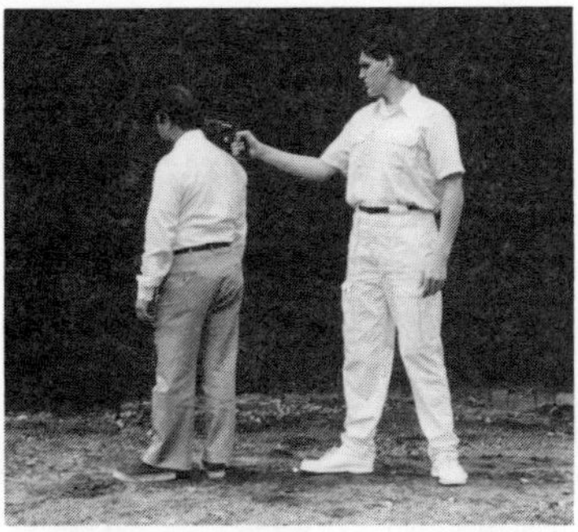

Figure 264

Figure 265

Figure 266

Figure 267

Figure 268

Figure 269

Five

Your opponent can carry a gun in many ways. He can carry it on the left or right hip, in the hollow of his back, or in a shoulder or ankle holster. No matter how he carries his gun, however, your first critical move is to prevent him from completing his draw. This may not be possible, because he normally will have the advantage of the first move. Fortunately, all is not lost. You can still prevent him from *aiming* the gun.

In Figure 270, the opponent is able to reach for and draw his gun. Step in quickly to the right and deliver two simultaneous blows: one, a right uppercut to the ribs; the other, a left palmheel to the gun hand (Figure 271). The palmheel will prevent him from aiming his gun, while the uppercut to the ribs will stun him long enough for you to close the distance.

Pull up your left foot and slam the opponent's right ear with your left hand (Figure 272), which will further stun him. While his ear is still ringing, step in with your left foot and capture his neck with a clothesline (Figure 273).

Step forward with your right foot and pull on both ends of the rope (Figure 274). The rope will now cut into the opponent's neck. Jerk the rope to bring him down.

Remember not to release the rope when you hit the opponent. A palmheel strike will open up your hand. However, a pinching action with your thumb and index finger will enable you to continue holding the rope.

Figure 270

Figure 271

Figure 272

Figure 273

Figure 274

Six

A rifle is more difficult for an opponent to handle. Once the rifle is hit to the side, it will be difficult to re-aim. However, the initial strike to the opponent's hand must be followed quickly with powerful blows that will both stun him and enable you to close the distance with little risk.

In Figure 275, the opponent aims a rifle at your chest. Keep calm; relax. Then move!

Twist your body to the side. Simultaneously, step in with your left foot to the outside of the rifle and grab the opponent's right hand with your left hand (Figure 276). Having swept the rifle to the side, strike him with a right palmheel to the solar plexus (Figure 277). At the same time, keep control over the gun with your left hand (Figure 278).

Do not let up on your attack. Smash the opponent with a backfist to the side of his neck (Figure 279). This will further stun him and will allow you time to make the capture. Draw a clockwise loop with the right end of the rope over, then around the opponent's head (Figures 280, 281). Complete the capture (Figure 282). At this point, the rope will cut the opponent's mouth. Take up the slack on the rope by punching energetically with your right hand (Figure 283).

The key to the successful capture is your first strike and the initial closing of the distance. However, the multiple attacks that follow are also important to keep the opponent from re-aiming his rifle. Remember, while drawing the clockwise loop around the opponent's head, you must keep control over his rifle with your left hand. Also, try to keep your shoulder in contact with his shoulder so you can feel his movements. Control over the rifle hand must be absolute. Otherwise, he might use the rifle as a club.

Figure 275

Figure 276

Figure 277

Figure 278

Figure 279

Figure 280

Figure 281

Figure 282

Figure 283

Seven

The opponent aims a rifle at your lower back (Figure 284). Do not tense your body. Any preparatory motion could make him pull the trigger.

Quickly twist your body clockwise to get out of the rifle's line of fire. At the time you turn, make contact with the side of the rifle with your elbow, thereby spoiling the opponent's aim. Step back with your right foot and hit the opponent's right hand with your right hand (Figure 285). Pivoting on your right foot, continue turning clockwise and step forward with your left foot. At the same time, grab the back of the opponent's neck with your left hand (Figure 286). This hit will force him to lower his head.

Keep firm control over the back of his neck with your left hand. Follow up quickly with a right palm-heel to the mouth. At this time, grip the opponent's left ear with the free fingers of your left hand. Do not release the left end of the rope (Figure 287).

Do not assume that the opponent is no longer dangerous. His finger is still on the trigger. Hit him in the eyes with the crook of your elbow (Figure 288). This will temporarily blind him and will further stun him. This strike will also bring the rope closer to his neck.

Draw a counterclockwise loop with the right end of the rope over, then around the opponent's head to complete the loop (Figure 289). Pull with the right end of the rope and punch with the left end (Figure 290). This will take up the slack, and the rope will hit his throat with a jerk. The pull and the punch should be in the same plane to have maximum effect. Should the opponent swing wildly with the rifle, be prepared to step back with your right foot and pull energetically on both ends of the rope to subdue him.

Figure 284

Figure 285

Figure 286

Figure 287

Figure 288

Figure 289

Figure 290